RYAN KIRBY

The
Embrace

EDITED BY:
BENJAMIN SLEDGE

PRODUCED BY:

HeartSupport, Inc.
411 West Monroe Street, #28
Austin, TX 78704
info@heartsupport.com
www.heartsupport.com

For my wife, parents, and band

CONTENTS

Preface   viii

1. Conditional Trust   1
   Day 1 Reflection   4
   Notes   5
2. Fear, Love, and Punishment   6
   Day 2 Reflection   9
   Notes   10
3. Fatherly Discipline   11
   Day 3 Reflection   14
   Notes   15
4. A Cosmic Dictator?   16
   Day 4 Reflection   19
   Notes   20
5. The Tech Crutch   21
   Day 5 Reflection   24
   Notes   25
6. Debtors   26
   Day 6 Reflection   29
   Notes   30
7. God In The Midst Of Mayhem   31
   Day 7 Reflection   34
   Notes   35
8. A One Woman Well   36
   Day 8 Reflection   39
   Notes   40
9. Conquer With Community   41
   Day 9 Reflection   44
   Notes   45
10. Man On God's Throne   46
    Day 10 Reflection   48

Notes	49
11. False Confidence	50
Day 11 Reflection	53
Notes	54
12. Blinded By Darkness	55
Day 12 Reflection	57
Notes	58
13. Be Careful Who You Listen To	59
Day 13 Reflection	62
Notes	63
14. The Idol of Image	64
Day 14 Reflection	67
Notes	68
15. Of Judgment, Slander, and Grace	69
Day 15 Reflection	72
Notes	73
16. Itching Ears And Secondary Passions	74
Day 16 Reflection	77
Notes	78
17. Foolish Dogma	79
Day 17 Reflection	82
Notes	83
18. Reflections On "Unwholesome Talk"	84
Day 18 Reflection	87
Notes	88
19. Like-Minded	89
Day 19 Reflection	92
Notes	93
20. Blind Guides	94
Day 20 Reflection	96
Notes	97
21. Willful Prayer	98
Day 21 Reflection	101
Notes	102

About the Author   103
About HeartSupport   104
Also By HeartSupport: Mountains   105
Also By HeartSupport: Dwarf Planet   106
Also By HeartSupport: ReWrite   107

PREFACE

I've struggled with my emotions for most of my life. By nature I'm an introvert who's more apt to stay closed off than to share deep feelings.

I haven't read a book in years, yet here I am writing a book about some of my most difficult memories and emotions. Life is funny like that.

If you're just picking up this book and don't know who I am or what HeartSupport does, the contents inside may seem odd for a devotional. HeartSupport—the nonprofit organization that published this workbook—works directly in the hard rock and metal music industry, providing fans the resources they need to overcome adversity and find healing. My friend Jake Luhrs founded the organization. He sings (though some would call it screaming) in a band named August Burns Red. I sing (scream) for a band called Fit For A King, and we often tour together.

Recently, Jake asked if I'd be willing to write a devotional to help men and women grow past their hurts, doubts, and struggles. My immediate reaction was, "No way! That's not for me! That's for people who've had *real* hardship in their lives. My life has been easy, and what I struggle with isn't what others deal with." Since becoming a touring musician, I've heard story after story—from different cultures and countries—that made me feel like my issues were trivial by comparison.

After a few weeks passed, Jake's proposition continued to haunt my thoughts. He sent multiple texts asking if I was interested. I didn't respond. After some time, I realized the reason I couldn't commit to the project was because it scared me. I was scared to think of how others would view my life story and fears—both of which I'd been hiding for years. Despite the adversity and pain I conquered years ago, I was afraid people would judge me. But deep down, I knew this was something I had to do for my healing, so I finally relented and let Jake know I was in.

I think most of us feel that what we're going through is unique, or that others will downplay the events, trauma, or struggles we're facing. When we feel our pain is meaningless, or that others have it worse, those small things can become mountains. Many in the Christian faith feel the need to look pretty or to minimize the areas where they're weak and need help. Authentic Christians, however, are honest about where they're *actively* failing—not just about their past sins.

While there has been healing in my life, I want this book to present a flawed man in need of additional change to continue to close the gap between me and Jesus.

I want to thank my wife, Crystal, and Ben Sledge, for making my bad grammar—and sometimes incoherent ramblings—make sense and become digestible. I want to thank my bandmates, Jared, Tuck, Daniel, and Bob for being my second family on the road, as well as the Fit For A King team: Cory, Adam, and Matt. They've all helped the band reach heights I never thought possible, which has led me to this moment.

Above all, I want to thank my family, including my wife, who I'll thank for a second time because she deserves it. We've each grown so much since some of the material in this book occurred. I'm so proud of the people you've become.

Finally, no matter what you've done or been through, the most important premise you need to grasp before we begin is this: *Jesus loves you.*

1

CONDITIONAL TRUST

"Give all your worries and cares to God, for he cares about you."
—1 Peter 5:7 (NLT)

Growing up, my life resembled a TV sitcom. My upbringing was easy, and my life remained free of major tragedy. Meanwhile, my high school friends seemed to go through horrendous circumstances. I knew friends who lost parents and loved ones. Their family lives consisted of divorce, toxic breakups, and addiction. None of their struggles seemed relevant to me. My parents were happily married (and remain so), my life was devoid of any serious romantic relationships, and the ones I had never ended in heartbreak. I thought little of death and mortality, because I hadn't lost anyone close to me.

Sure, I had my personal teenage angst dealing with loneliness, social anxiety, and low self-esteem, but those issues never ate me up. Even expressing those struggles seemed silly. Why should I bother friends—let alone God—

with such insignificant issues, when everyone else dealt with *real* issues?

My strategy to keep those emotions bottled up worked well throughout the rest of high school and the beginning of college. Burying my issues was easy and made me appear low-maintenance. Looking back though, the only reason I could bury anything was because of the loving support from my parents and my community. They kept me going, whether or not I knew it.

I was just shy of turning twenty years old when I joined my band, Fit For A King, which is when things began to unravel. We were a large local band and had aspirations to become something more, but, because of my lack of confidence, I convinced myself we'd never move beyond playing home shows. Even though I was the frontman for a band, I was still attending college full-time. But I put little effort into my studies, because I was focused on the band. My parents noticed this trend and suggested I go all in with the band or with school. The condition for going all in with the band required me to find a full-time job, however. With these two options laid out before me, and my parents' support, I chose music; but finding a job eluded me.

After a few months, I became desperate to find work. Any job I applied for wouldn't allow me to take time off for the occasional tour. But, as luck would have it, a fan of the band named Josiah—who later became one of my best friends— offered me a job with a flooring company. The catch? I had to move to Oklahoma. Josiah even offered me a bedroom at his house where I could live for next to nothing. This was too sweet to pass up. I packed up my belongings and moved out of state, away from friends, family, and, most importantly, my community.

For the first time, I was alone. Lacking community, I had to face all the issues I'd been burying for years. Everything I deemed "insignificant" came rising to the surface. Over ten years of stifled emotion, pain, and struggle overwhelmed me, to the point where I didn't want to get out of bed most days. I would talk to any girl on the internet willing to give me attention, watch porn on repeat, and eat junk food. Things would have gotten darker had it not been for Josiah, another friend named Clint, and my parents. But I still left God out of the picture; I was determined to handle these issues on my own.

After a few months, I finally turned to God and brought everything out into the open. If I'm honest, it didn't feel like he was listening. After all, I'd made a mess of my life. That's a common misconception, though. We often expect our lives to get instantly better once we turn our cares and burdens over to Christ. That wasn't the case for me, and, for most others, I'm willing to bet instant change didn't happen either. However, I took that first scary step of giving control over to God.

1 Peter 5:7 often reminds me that a first step begins by turning *all* things over to God. Turning over *all* my issues was something I struggled with for the longest time, but it was the key to changing my life. It became the prison key that unlocked me from my cell and opened me up to love. Imagine if I had trusted God's word earlier! So many walls and defenses wouldn't have been built.

So, today, give *all* your worries to the Lord, not just the ones you deem worthy. To him, they *all* matter.

DAY 1 REFLECTION

1. Have you ever felt that something you're going through isn't important enough to bother God? How about bringing it up to others?
2. What would happen if your support system was suddenly removed? Who would you turn to?

2

FEAR, LOVE, AND PUNISHMENT

"There is no fear in love, but perfect love casts out fear. For fear has to do with punishment, and whoever fears has not been perfected in love."

—1 John 4:18 (ESV)

G rowing up, I was afraid of God, rather than feeling loved by him. This was strange, given that church people told me God was love, while constantly reminding me of what God said I *could* and *couldn't* do. The warnings of punishment that awaited me when I broke "rules" kept me in a perpetual state of fear, so I found myself more scared of, than feeling loved by, God.

The message in many churches focuses more on hell than on God's unconditional love for sinners—at least, that's what has stood out to me. So the focus of most Christians will then become, "Get it together, or face eternal suffering," as opposed to, "You are so infinitely loved, Christ died for you and has hope even when you fail."

When I became a Christian, it was less my decision than

one forced on me as a young child, as I wasn't yet sure what Christianity entailed. I knew my parents wanted me to come to the same belief, and pastors reaffirmed this by reminding young children that if they didn't want to suffer eternally in a lake of fire apart from mommy and daddy, then they must accept Jesus.

There was just one major problem—fear drove me to God, *not love.* When you think about this situation logically, any relationship based on fear is one our friends and family members would tell us to avoid. We use terms like *abusive* and *manipulative* when describing relationships governed by fear. Therefore, why on earth would the most intimate relationship you're supposed to have, the one with your Creator, be one based on fear?

As fear was the foundation for my belief and adoration, my relationship with God became shaky and disconnected.

By my teenage years, my fear had turned into apathy, because I felt I had already messed up too many times. Since going to hell was a realistic possibility for me, even if I attempted to get back on track, I knew I'd stumble again. *So why bother?* Why not live how I wanted to *now* and deal with God later?

To comfort myself, I still considered myself a Christian, as it provided a sense of relief not to deny God outright through my words. My actions and thoughts, however, told a different story. God was never on my mind. I never prayed or practiced spiritual disciplines, and I certainly didn't consider what God wanted for me or my future. I lived most of my life this way, even as the frontman for my band.

In 2013, though, I had a wake-up call. I received a message from a fan thanking me for the music the band created. This wasn't uncommon, but this message turned out different. My jaw dropped when I read the line, "Your lyrics brought me to God this year. I wanted to thank you for that." While the lyrics I wrote were about God and other life struggles, I never imagined something I'd done would help someone find faith. At the same time, that moment also showed me how far I had strayed. Spreading God's Word wasn't my goal. My goal was to write catchy songs with a Christian meaning, just so I could feel close to God. The whole process was an attempt to make me feel better about myself while I lived out a functional atheism based on fear.

This became a turning point in my relationship with Jesus. Like the Apostle John teaches, love casts out fear. If I seek God's love, and not crawl to him in fear, then I'll meet the real Jesus, not the Zeus figure I'd been taught was waiting to catch me in sin.

This revelation came quickly that day, but the road to relationship wasn't easy. It took time, and I had to believe 1 John 4:18. "Fear has to do with punishment," John reminds us. If we base our relationship with God on fear, the apostle reminds us we've got it all wrong. We don't understand God, and we certainly don't understand love.

What will it take for you today to choose God's love over a perverted message of fear? Don't spend years like I did believing a false message. Instead, embrace God's unconditional love for you today, and watch yourself become perfected in love.

DAY 2 REFLECTION

1. Is your relationship with God fueled by a fear of hell, or by his love?
2. Does your spiritual environment focus more on God's wrath or on his love? How can you surround yourself with a community that spurs you on to be complete in love?

3

FATHERLY DISCIPLINE

"For the moment all discipline seems painful rather than pleasant, but later it yields the peaceful fruit of righteousness to those who have been trained by it."
—Hebrews 12:11 (ESV)

I got busted watching porn when I was roughly fourteen years old.

The grounding my father gave me lasted from my freshman year until my senior year of high school. My computer became off limits and the grounding was "indefinite," because I found ways around my father's parameters or through Myspace. Most of my punishment and groundings were well deserved (okay... maybe *all* of them). Today, I know my father disciplined me out of love and to keep me from harm, but at the time it felt like I was constantly blowing it. I often thought my Dad's love was contingent on obedience. Much like I talked about earlier, I began to view God this way, too.

My dad is a good dad. Unlike some people experience, he

never drank or was physically abusive, and he always treated my mom with respect. However, he stumbled along figuring out how to be an effective parent. He grew up without a father, and I was his first child, so he did the best he could.

My issues stemmed from the fact that I always thought he was disappointed in or upset with me, rather than delighting in me. I never opened up to him about my struggles, because I assumed they'd be met with righteous anger.

That's why he caught me watching porn. I didn't want to tell him about my guilt, since he'd be furious. I also didn't tell him I lost my virginity at the age of seventeen, for the same reason. Had I told him, there would just be an indefinite grounding; and when I got caught, that only solidified my beliefs.

Much of our relationship revolved around me screwing up, getting grounded, and there being no real conversation or lesson, aside from, "Don't *ever* do that again. You're grounded indefinitely." I wanted those moments to have been teaching points and to have had deep, vulnerable conversation with my dad, but the lesson instead became, "Damn. I got grounded, and this sucks. I gotta be more careful next time."

It's easy to see how when you have an earthly father who isn't perfect, you view God the same way. While my father didn't execute discipline the way I wanted, as I've grown older, I've seen he wanted to save me from a lot of heartbreak. When kids aren't disciplined, they turn into spoiled brats who believe the world revolves around their needs and wants. I'm sure we all know at least one person like that. If they're disciplined too harshly without explanation or gentleness, then they hide their missteps.

With God, though, we have a loving, perfect father who

will discipline us because he loves us. That probably sounds harsh right? Even this verse sounds harsh, but it's true. Without being corrected when we're falling short, we're left traveling a path toward our own implosion. Imagine if God left all your character flaws unchecked. Then imagine the same for those around you. That would be the very definition of hell, wouldn't it? Selfish, greedy, addicted, hurtful men and women would be left to continue growing more self-centered and destructive.

We must remember that God's love requires discipline, but that it's fair and for our own good. It's not that there's a standard we can't achieve and therefore get punished for failing to meet; but that, because he loves us, Christ wants to see us grow to our full potential and become humble, open to correction, and loving.

DAY 3 REFLECTION

1. Have you ever gotten busted and disciplined, only to later become glad you did? Why?
2. Do you hold any resentment toward parents or authority figures because of the way they issued discipline? Do you think that's transferred over to your view of God?

4

A COSMIC DICTATOR?

"But because of his great love for us, God, who is rich in mercy, made us alive with Christ even when we were dead in transgressions—it is by grace you have been saved."
—Ephesians 2:4-5 (NIV)

W hile on tour, after I play a show, I chat with people at our merch table. Most of our conversations revolve around generic statements like, "Great show!" or questions as to why I didn't play a certain song. However, there are sometimes conversations that stick like glue. The most recent one to happen was in December 2018 when I was playing a venue in Minneapolis. *(Fun fact: Varsity Theatre is the name of the venue and known for the best public restrooms in America. Google for an image.)* After the line died down at the table, I noticed a man in his late thirties waiting awkwardly in a nearby corner.

When we talked, he shared about how his life revolved around fear and God. He believed he had let God down, wasn't worthy of heaven, and that eternal torment in hell was his final destination. Each time I would try to assuage those fears and speak about Jesus and a God of love, he became combative. He'd share about the times he repeatedly stole in high school and college, how he was sleeping with his girlfriend, or how he cursed more and more each day. While explaining his failures, he began to cry.

While I sat listening to the man, I couldn't help but think, "Man, what person *did this* to you? What church made you believe God is a cold and unforgiving tyrant? Because everything you're describing about a so-called God of love I wouldn't wish on my worst enemy."

My final attempt to lean in and crush this distorted thinking was by explaining the gospel—that nothing you've done or will ever do can separate you from God's love. The cross covers all shortcomings, past and present, and Christ believes you can grow even when you keep falling down.

His response to the gospel—the main tenets of the Christian faith—was, "Well, at my church..."

It finally clicked, and I found the answer to his pain. The man explained that the version of God his church had taught resembled a dictator. Love was conditional, because forgiveness was for those who followed the "rules" to a T. Even more disturbing was that the man hadn't attended church in over a decade, but he was still plagued by fear because of what the church and his parents had emphasized.

I didn't change his mind or get anywhere with him that night, so I signed his CD with the verse in this devotional (Ephesians 2:4-5). Before he left, I told him to read that verse any time he felt God didn't love or wouldn't forgive him.

I haven't heard from him since, but the memory stings. I often wonder if he's found God's love instead of wrath. It's sad that so many have been burned by churches and told a story of a God that the Pharisees of Scripture would relate to more than the character and personhood of Jesus.

Christians often believe God's love is conditional because that's what we see in our lives and relationships. Yet this verse reminds us that while we were dead in our transgressions, God wanted to bestow rich mercies on us. And he continues to do so every day.

Each day we must remind ourselves of a God of love who has, not condemnation for us, but "rich mercies." *Even when we find ourselves dead in sin*. Lean into the knowledge of his love today, and let it transform your heart.

DAY 4 REFLECTION

1. How do you view God? As a cruel taskmaster or as a loving father? Maybe even somewhere in-between? How do you think you came to view him this way?
2. Have you ever felt as if you had let God down so many times that you can't believe he would still continue to love you? If so, why?

5

THE TECH CRUTCH

"But godliness with contentment is great gain. For we brought nothing into the world, and we can take nothing out of it."
—1 Timothy 6:6-7 (NIV)

It's easy to spot other people's "crutches." Crutches are what we turn to for pain relief or when we feel overwhelmed, stressed, or just want to escape. For some people that can be sex, alcohol, drugs, or social media. Even binging on Netflix is easy to spot as a crutch in this day and age when we want to escape. As someone who adheres to a straight edge lifestyle—meaning I consume no alcohol or drugs—, my crutch was a blind spot. If there's one thing all these years of touring have taught me, it's that *everyone* has a crutch—*especially* me.

When I moved to Oklahoma and found myself feeling alienated, I developed a crutch I didn't deal with until recently. For most of my life, I've never been content with my possessions, and that evolved into a tech obsession. Gadgets, computers, games, it didn't matter what the type of tech was, I wanted it all (or at least to try it all). Instead of filling the emptiness with God during the time away from my family, I filled it with materialism.

The thing about materialism is that it's subversive and has crept into our churches. We want pastors to entertain us, worship songs to be about what we feel or like, or kids' programs to spoon-feed our children. They need to be tech savvy, serve coffee to keep us awake, and if the service doesn't fill the void where God is supposed to be, we believe the church isn't doing their job, because we—selfishly—aren't feeling closer to God. Once you've bought into materialism and consumerism, the behavior becomes easy to rationalize, and we become defensive.

While filling that void didn't come from demanding something out of a church, drugs, or alcohol, I demanded it out of the tech I bought. No joke, there was a year when I had twelve phones. *Twelve!* My wife, Crystal, tried to point out how ridiculous this was, but, like most everyone does, I got defensive and rationalized the behavior: "It's a hobby. There's nothing wrong with that."

Until this last year, these issues have persisted. Each day is still a constant battle to remind myself, You don't need this." I've made small progress and even kept the phone I have for a year. That may sound small and absurd, but I haven't kept a phone for over a year in nine years.

The verse we read for this devotional has been particularly helpful for me in combating my materialism crutch. The Apostle Paul reminds us that there is great gain and contentment to be found in godliness (i.e., seeking God and his will and way). Then he reminds us of the obvious:

"You came into the world naked and with nothing, and everything you own you can't take with you."

When we turn to things that aren't God, we're always left wanting. We try to shove trinkets into the gaping hole, and for a season we can feel better. But then we return to feeling lonely, upset, or empty. The cycle then repeats, and I'm off buying a new phone or laptop to quell the anguish, even though I know that true contentment can only come in the form of Christ.

I'm not sure it's possible for us to live without a crutch in this world, so instead of turning to the things that leave us empty, let's turn to the only crutch that can give us life to the fullest.

DAY 5 REFLECTION

1. Simple and to the point—what's *your* crutch? The answer can't be, "Nothing," as we all lean on things other than God. Dig deep.
2. Has giving into your crutch ever resulted in sustainable happiness? How can you trust God to become the crutch you lean into?

6

DEBTORS

"Let no debt remain outstanding, except the continuing debt to love one another, for whoever loves others has fulfilled the law."
—Romans 13:8 (NIV)

When I moved to Oklahoma, I didn't have a lot of money. The money I had—as I stated from yesterday's devotional reading—I spent on tech. Even though I didn't have the money to pay for the phones and computers, I never let that stop me. Instead, I did what most Americans do when they want they can't afford: I opened up credit cards.

For a while I could manage my debts and even appeared responsible (Dave Ramsey is laughing at me somewhere). I was eighteen, living at home, and had a job at a fast food joint. I remember buying a computer monitor from Fry's Electronics with a credit card and paying it off two weeks later. But by the time I arrived in Oklahoma at age twenty-one, I had new bills. Rent and food all add up when they're no longer free, and I wasn't making that much more than I had at my fast food job.

So what did I do to support my tech obsession? I opened up *more* credit cards and went on Best Buy shopping sprees and Amazon binges, and I racked up debt on any other web site that would let me put off paying. I even tried selling some of the twelve phones I owned, but that still left me $100 to $300 short after each sale. Without fail, I put myself in a revolving door of debt. I'd love to say I curbed my spending habits by the time the band took off, but I just kept spending. In fact, by the time I turned twenty-seven, I had accumulated $20,000 in debt! On average, I was paying $400 a month toward my debt, which was more than the cost of my car bill.

Imagine getting married and having to explain to your spouse that you owe $20,000 in debt because you have zero impulse control and spend your earnings on superficial trinkets. I thank God my wife didn't have an aneurysm when she found out about my stupid and unproductive debt.

So much of my life revolved around personal satisfaction in these purchases, instead of lovingly pouring my money and energy into other people. That's what this verse reminds us to do. When we put our energy into acquiring debt, we're searching for happiness in places it can't be found. Instead, my time and energy needed to go toward loving and serving others, as the Apostle Paul reminds the Roman church. This verse has continually struck home when I'm tempted to make new purchases or have lapses in judgement about spending. I often have felt I let God down (as well as Dave Ramsey, ha), and I could see the frustration my debts caused my wife. But I also have to remember God is loving and kind and wants to see me free of debt.

I have owed God a debt, but he wiped that clean through Jesus's substitution on the cross. Earthly debt is a reminder that we need not owe others our entire life, because then we become slaves. Instead, like Paul reminds us, when we carry no debt—financial or even personal—we love ourselves and others, and we fulfill the law.

DAY 6 REFLECTION

1. How has pouring out your time, energy, or finances affected those around you? How about your relationship with God?
2. Are you indebted to someone? Do you have a plan to settle that debt? What steps can you take to begin settling that debt?

7

GOD IN THE MIDST OF MAYHEM

"So do not fear, for I am with you; do not be dismayed, for I am your God. I will strengthen you and help you; I will uphold you with my righteous right hand."
—Isaiah 41:10 (NIV)

The time between age twenty and twenty-four was a critical point in my life, which I why I keep bringing it up. That period of my life was when my internal struggles from my teenage years began to manifest.

I wasn't the "hormonal teenager" that ended up acting out and making poor decisions, but I certainly had my fair share of failures. I didn't sleep around as a teenager, and I stayed a virgin until my senior year of high school, but I did enjoy spending time on Myspace—*especially* talking to girls on Myspace. I never believed these actions would plant seeds of lust in my mind, given that I was busy playing music with friends, which often took my mind off women—but they did.

Things finally came to a head when I moved away and the distractions were no longer around. Lust became a source of entertainment and escape. Once away from family and friends, I began texting or talking to girls on social media—anyone I could flirt with or who would reciprocate the attention. Because I lived in a small town of 9,000 people in Oklahoma, I could never act on impulse, given that so many of the girls lived hours and states away. Interactions remained words—until I began supplementing them with pornography.

Like most Christians trying to justify our sin, I kept telling myself, "This is better than sleeping around," or, "God would *prefer* me looking at porn over having actual sex." The justification only filled me further to the brim with emptiness and loneliness. Flirting and porn became such a routine, I knew of no way to break free of them, even when I wanted to quit. I felt worthless and believed no girl would want a single twenty-something who was living in Oklahoma and making only $150 a week. Not to mention I was in an unsigned band that traveled often. But even though I felt dismayed, God was at work.

When times are tough, we often wonder, "How can God possibly be at work amid my brokenness, sin, and struggle?" Like this verse says, we fear, we feel dismayed, and we have no idea how God will uphold his righteous hand and strengthen us, let alone get us out of the holes we've dug for ourselves. Instead of taking this verse at face value, we crumble and continue to have a pessimistic outlook on our lives and futures, because all we can see is the struggle.

One evening, our band played a show in Rogers, Arkansas. The show ended pretty badly. The local opening act ate our catering food, there were only about twenty people in attendance, and we had a bunch of technical difficulties.

I noticed a cute, but shy, young woman sitting at one of the other band's merch tables. Mentally berating myself, I assumed she had to be the girlfriend of one of the members of a local band, so I didn't speak with her (we made eye contact, though). The next day, however, I got a friend request from her. I was elated until I saw my assumption was correct —she did have a boyfriend. I later discovered her boyfriend had mistakenly logged into her account and thought he added me as a friend through his profile. Strange? Sure. Divine? Maybe.

I messaged her quickly, since my status quo was to flirt with girls online. Within the message I sent, I gave her my number in case she "ever wanted to text." Despite my struggles and shadiness, God took that moment and used it for something good that would transform my life. Not long after, the girl I messaged on Facebook broke up with her boyfriend, and I received a text.

That woman would become my wife, Crystal.

Don't get me wrong, I was still very broken and lonely. God didn't fix me overnight, and healing was a long process. In fact, it only got worse before it got better (as you'll learn about in tomorrow's reading).

Despite my struggle, pain, and hurt, looking back now I can see how God has strengthened me even when I felt dismayed. Perhaps he's doing the same for you today, even if you don't realize it.

DAY 7 REFLECTION

1. Have you or do you make excuses for sinful behavior? If so, why?
2. Do you believe God can take your brokenness and strengthen your life, resulting in change? What do you think is keeping you from trusting him more?

8

A ONE WOMAN WELL

"You should be faithful to your wife, just as you take water from your own well. And don't be like a stream from which just any woman may take a drink."
—Proverbs 5:15-16 (CEV)

Remember yesterday when I said things got worse before they got better? My relationship with Crystal took a nosedive and started one of the most shame-inducing periods of my life. To this day, I still lament my behavior.

Everything started innocently enough, as it usually does in a new relationship. Crystal and I began talking, and with time became "Facebook official" as boyfriend and girlfriend. I was happy; I had never felt loved by another woman (in a romantic kind of way) until we met. Our biggest obstacle, however, became the distance between us. Crystal lived four hours away in Arkansas and often sacrificed her time to drive to see me. Being fully seen and loved like that made me feel whole. It could have been perfect—*had it not been for me.*

During our time apart, I rushed back into old habits,

which made having a romantic relationship impossible. Without parsing words, I need to confess what a horrible boyfriend I was until our engagement. I still made it a point to text—on occasion even flirting—with girls I had spoken with prior to my relationship with Crystal. Oh, I knew that what I was doing was wrong, but I continued to try to justify my actions, since I wasn't physically cheating.

In addition to this behavior, I refused to be supportive of Crystal. When we'd talk on the phone and she'd vent—because she wanted me to listen and hear about her life—I would think, "Man, all she ever does is complain!" I didn't recognize that part of why she needed to vent was because of my behavior. With time, our relationship suffered because of my actions, and we broke up.

Want to guess what was the first thing I did when we broke up? I texted another girl. Disgusting, right?

That moment made me hit rock bottom and realize how awful I was. Knowing I'd blown a good relationship, I begged Crystal to take me back. God only knows why she did, given my behavior, but I'm grateful for that second chance. Once we rekindled our relationship, I deleted from my phone every number of any girl I'd had any inappropriate contact with. Whereas Crystal had committed to me from day one, I had to make a choice to change my behavior and commit fully to Crystal.

Not long after I made that commitment, we got engaged. As of my writing this, we've been together for over four years.

The scripture you read today was *the* verse that made me realize I wanted to commit. In our culture, it's easy to justify fishing around the pond and seeing what your options are, especially when you're not married. The thing is, though,

Crystal *became* my spouse, and my actions and emotional infidelity damaged our relationship. Giving myself over to others was just a cheap imitation for the intimacy I found with her. Even prior to dating Crystal, all the parts of myself I gave to other women, I didn't get to give fully to my wife, and to this day that bothers me.

A little context for this passage makes it easier to see why this matters. King Solomon wrote Proverbs and is known as one of the wisest men in history. Yet he had over seven hundred wives and three hundred concubines. He obviously had a problem giving himself to many women. But Proverbs contains instructions for his sons; he shares wisdom he gained from age and his mistakes. If anyone knew why it was important to commit to one woman and not drink from other wells, it was Solomon.

Today, many of us can easily bounce from person to person, with all the apps available at our fingertips. I'd hate for you to experience the pain I went through, and I believe Solomon would say the same. Don't let your relationship bottom out before it's forced to get better. Make the wise decision, and be honorable and loyal to the person you're with.

DAY 8 REFLECTION

1. Do you have trouble committing to relationships? How about plans or friendships? Do you think you have a fear that you'll miss out on something better?
2. As sexualized as our culture is, do you find it hard to be loyal to one person? Do you often find yourself on apps? What do you think is the reason for that? Do you trust that God's way and plans are best for you?

9

CONQUER WITH COMMUNITY

"Though one may be overpowered, two can defend themselves. A cord of three strands is not quickly broken."
—Ecclesiastes 4:12 (NIV)

Crystal and I have experienced our fair share of challenges in our marriage, but we've been lucky enough to never break up (except for maybe an hour). Having someone watch your back and fight through the trials you face in life is a blessing, but it can't be just my wife and me against the world. If I'm honest, we've both struggled to make God and community the center of our marriage. We both love Jesus, and our faith has never wavered, but prioritizing our relationship with him has proved difficult because of our jobs.

Crystal is a flight attendant, and I'm a touring musician, which makes having time at home rare. As I write today's devotional, Crystal has been at work the past few days in different cities away from home. Due to scheduling that is out of her control, she also works most Sundays, whereas I'm on tour six or more months a year, so finding a home church has been hard.

Truthfully, we both haven't tried very hard, and we have made a lot of excuses. Crystal and I are both introverts who struggle with social anxiety—odd, I know, for a musician and flight attendant. Because we interact with people all the time, it's the perfect storm of excuses as to why we don't commit to a home church and connect into a community.

There are also personal issues I had with a former church that play into the equation. So I tell myself, "It's not worth going. You'll just be leaving immediately anyway, so you'll never get tight with a community group, and you'll always be the outsider." There's truth to my thinking, though, which makes it easier to rationalize. If I were to join a community group and church, I wouldn't get to attend and see them every week, but that's missing the point isn't it? **Some community is better than none!**

There are always fans who invite me to their church when I'm touring, but I need to find a community I can vet and then connect into long-term. Sadly, not all churches are created equal, and some teach behavioral modification and threats of hell over God's infinite patience, love, and hope. But that's also just another excuse, when I should at the very least try going to one.

Ecclesiastes 4:12 reminds us that when we have community—people committed to seeing us grow in faith and love—we aren't as easily defeated when the suffering and hardships of this world come along. Sometimes Crystal and I disagree or fight. We even have the types of arguments that lead to a door or two being slammed. I need others to see where I've gone wrong or where I need to love more.

After those fights, I often ask, "Where was God in *that* argument? Would it have even gotten to this point if I had placed him at the center first?" If I don't place God at the center of my marriage, then I only get the cord of two strands. We might defend ourselves for a time, but even better is God at the center and a community of people wrapped around us to fend off trials when they come along.

What can you do today to fight off the attacks that come? If you aren't living in community and are making excuses like I am, what steps can you take to change that?

Remember, the more alone you are, the less defense you have. With Christ and fellow believers, however, you can begin to take on anything life throws at you.

DAY 9 REFLECTION

1. Do you have a community or a group of Christians from church that are able to rally around you when times get tough? If so, what benefits have you seen? If not, what excuses do you make to keep you from connecting?

2. Hebrews 10:25 (BSB) states ,"Let us not neglect meeting together, as some have made a habit." When you're not living connected or in community, what are the effects on your life? What steps can you take to correct that?

10

MAN ON GOD'S THRONE

"It is better to take refuge in the Lord than to trust in man."
　—Psalm 118:8 (ESV)

I think each person reading through this devotional has felt lost, caught in a fog, or not known what step to take next. Perhaps you're in the midst of feeling that way now. In my twenty-eight years on this earth, I can honestly say I have felt this way for twenty-three of them. It was like wandering around in the dark, but not because life threw me a bunch of curveballs. I had my eyes closed and refused to open them. I used other Christians as an excuse to wander around that way and to block out God.

For most of my life, I was the church attendee who scoffed at the people stating that "God spoke to [them]." This phrase —more often than not—is overused and abused (I'm looking at you, folks who use God as an excuse during a breakup!). I would roll my eyes anytime someone prefaced a statement with that phrase. I viewed it as a cop-out when people could justify their actions with the logic, "God told me to do it, therefore you can't question it." Even now, I still believe people use God as an excuse or a shield as opposed to dealing with hard truths and uncomfortable situations.

However, this outlook created a barrier in my relationship to God, and I began having a difficult time hearing his voice. I pinned the actions of church members and other Christians on God, thus creating an imperfect and unfavorable view of the most loving being. This warped outlook is the number one issue I see people have with Christianity. When people share their beef with the Christian faith, it's always "someone did this" or "someone hurt me." They highlight their mistreatment by other Christians or the Church, *not* God.

Circling back around to why I wandered in the dark, my perspective was the same as those offended by other Christians. I would tune them out and discount almost anything the church said. This was largely in part to the way I saw them projecting personal desires or behavioral modification onto others. It even led me to become hesitant to read the Bible. All these roadblocks interfered in my ability to hear God, because I had put people on God's throne.

Finally, after years of feeling lost, I recognized I was the one closing off my relationship with God because of the actions of imperfect people, when I had a loving father who would never let me down. I opened my heart back up, and though sometimes the future feels blurry, instead of trusting in man, I can hear him leading me. When we let down our walls and trust in God as opposed to man, our path—and life —become a lot more fruitful and clear.

Are you unable to hear God because you put people on his throne? If so, it's time to remove them and open your heart back up to the one who truly loves and cares for you.

DAY 10 REFLECTION

1. Where have you most felt let down in life? By God? Or by other people? In the Twelve Steps of Alcoholics Anonymous, they have people write out lists of those who've wronged them, but they also own their selfish actions. Write a list of ways you've been hurt or wounded by people. Then write a list of hurts you feel came from God. I think you'll be surprised at the answers and connections.

2. What makes you feel most fulfilled? Money? Being in a relationship? Other people? A church? A job? What keeps you from taking refuge in the Lord?

11

FALSE CONFIDENCE

"But blessed is the one who trusts in the Lord, whose confidence is in him."
—Jeremiah 17:7 (NIV)

I don't want you to get the wrong impression from the previous entries, that I only deal with past struggles and sins. I still have plenty of battles I face daily—some old, some new. One of my current battles revolves around confidence and trust. I'd never describe myself as an overly confident person, but for most of my life I've had some level of mettle (aside from my social anxiety of course). However, within the last six months I have found my confidence slipping and my trust being laid in the wrong place. It ended up taking a mental toll on me and provided a much-needed wake-up call.

In the beginning of 2019, my band went on tour with August Burns Red. We'd only toured with them once before, in 2015, but in this go-round we were direct support to them as the headliner. It was an awesome confirmation to see things going in such a positive direction for my band. The tour was even the most financially successful one we've had, and the audience response was the best we've ever seen. I was on cloud nine and excited about the future, my confidence soaring.

Then we hopped on a European tour the following month with the band Emmure.

Our band has toured Europe only a couple of times, and we're *significantly* less well-known overseas than in North America. I understood the response and finances wouldn't be as positive as what we'd just been through with August Burns Red—*and they weren't*. We broke even on costs and on profit. As you grow older as a band, that's a hard pill to swallow, especially when you leave your wife for a month and come home with no money to show for it. The crowds were dismal, and even their reaction was maybe ten percent of what we received stateside. Although I *knew* the tour would be like this, I fell into a deep rut. To be honest, my emotional state might have bordered on depression, but I hesitate to call it that.

That tour brought me from cloud nine to the lowest I've felt about the band in years, and I'm still feeling the effects. My confidence in myself and the band has been low. But that's also part of the problem. I put my confidence and trust in myself and success, and I gave little credit to God. During the tour I spent very little time communing with Christ, even when things were going amazing on the August Burns Red headline. You'd think I'd show gratitude toward the one who gave me the success, but I made it about me.

The problem with putting ultimate confidence in yourself is that you'll fail. Because that's what humans do. We fail, fall, and stumble. However, when you place your trust in the

Lord, you'll find a strong foundation. That's why this verse in Jeremiah talks about placing your trust in God and not in yourself or other people.

This is still a process I'm working toward. Some days my trust is in me or success, and the next it's in God, but I know that trusting the Lord is the right path—the path that will fulfill me.

What are you placing your confidence in? A romantic relationship? Money? Success? Perhaps it's time to turn your will and way over to God and learn to trust him instead.

DAY 11 REFLECTION

1. Whether in the past or present, what have you put your trust in other than God? How did it turn out?
2. Complete this sentence: If I were to lose_____, then I would feel _____. Why do you feel this way? How can you learn to place your trust back in Christ?

12

BLINDED BY DARKNESS

"But the one who hates his brother is in the darkness and walks
in the darkness, and does not know where he is going because the
darkness has blinded his eyes."
—1 John 2:11 (NASB)

I'm a competitive person. I've always loved sports and video games where there's a clear winner and loser, even though I've never really succeeded at either.

My natural bent toward healthy rivalry has even benefitted me in my music career. I believe that's because being in a band is—by nature—a competition. Each night you're competing for new fans, the best set, and audience interaction. As our band grew from playing local shows to touring regionally, that competitive nature heated up. Once your band hits any level of success, then you have to compete for sales, too. There are bills to pay and families to feed. But any time money gets involved, the environment can get ugly.

Once money became a factor, I began to develop blind spots in my thinking. When we would have a bad night selling merchandise, I would default to blaming other bands and tearing down their performances. Sometimes I would even attack individual band members instead of reflecting on what I could do to improve my sales or my performance. I never maliciously slandered them, but I made little jabs like, "They sounded rough", or, "Their screaming didn't sound great." Worst of all, I never said these things to their faces, but only behind their backs. Even if they had asked me how their sets were, I would have lied. It was cowardly.

One night in 2016, my perspective changed. I heard another band member we were touring with making disparaging remarks about our band after they had a rough night. Naturally, I was upset. But as I thought about the remarks made about our band, I realized, "How can I be upset when I do the same to others? And how many people have overheard me?" As a Christian, I felt ashamed, as my actions were a poor reflection of God's love. Here I was, on tour with several non-Christians, mocking and belittling them because I was jealous, frustrated, or overly competitive.

When I read this verse in 1 John, my eyes opened. I knew my attitude and actions *had* to change. I was living in darkness while pretending to be a child of light.

Don't get me wrong: Competition can be healthy. But when you're using it to tear down others? Don't delude yourself. That benefits no one, and it only plants the seeds of envy and hatred for your fellow man.

If you hate your brother, you're walking around blind. Open your eyes to the light and see where you may be letting competition, envy, or hatred blind you.

DAY 12 REFLECTION

1. When have you torn down others or made jabs at them because you were jealous or frustrated? Did it change the situation, or did it just make you more bitter?
2. When you're tempted to bad-mouth another person, remember that Scripture teaches they're made in the image of God. What can you do to be a light to others you may resent and to speak life over them?

13

BE CAREFUL WHO YOU LISTEN TO

"Beloved, do not believe every spirit, but test the spirits to see whether they are from God, for many false prophets have gone out into the world."
—1 John 4:1 (ESV)

I assume that most people reading this devotional are Christians or at the very least grew up going to church at some point. Some of you may like my band or another band known for their Christianity. We forget, however, that most of our beliefs about church, God, and faith are shaped and formed by the churches we attend or the people we surround ourselves with. This isn't a bad thing. Community with fellow believers directly shapes us, and the gathering of saints in corporate worship is important, too. But for many in Western culture, our views may have never evolved from the ones we had when we were growing up. I believe that true discovery and authentic faith come through exploration and, as this verse states, "test[ing] the spirits to see whether they are from God."

For most of my life, my impressions, doctrines, beliefs, and views of Christianity came from a single church. I went there for over eighteen years with my parents. While I think it's important to stay committed to a church, it's important to recognize that churches often mimic the interpretations of Scripture and doctrine of a particular pastor. Some churches will only teach predestination, whereas others will only teach free will. Some teach women can be elders, whereas others teach the position is only for men. When you grow up in the same church and don't know any better, you tend to adopt the same beliefs. I guess that was part of my problem, because I never felt like my faith was my own, so there was a certain emptiness to it. I didn't know whether what the church was teaching was false. I just went along for the ride.

Within the last year, however, I've felt a massive shift and growth in my relationship with Christ. The main reason being that I began to reach out, explore, and hear differing viewpoints on theology and Christianity. There are always new and seductive false doctrines that emerge and viewpoints I disagree with, but there are other things I've learned that have completely changed my view of the Scriptures.

If your faith isn't your own, how can you grow? How will you decide what's false and what's not? Or what's opinion and what's truth?

Your relationship with God is like any other relationship. If it's not interesting, advancing, and growing in depth, then you'll have a tendency to grow apart or to watch the relationship suffer and become stale. Test the spirits instead, and get to know God. Absorb as much scripture as possible. Read the original texts and translations. Question what you've been taught—but in a healthy manner, because far too many throw their faith to the wayside instead of leaning into the discomfort.

The more you see what is of God, the more you'll be able to observe what's true or when you're being led astray by slick words or fancy preachers. Find *your* faith; don't just mimic the faith of other people.

DAY 13 REFLECTION

1. What views of Christianity do you hold currently? Would you be willing to have them challenged so you can grow, or would you resist? If there's resistance, explore why you feel that way.
2. Is your relationship with God growing or stagnating, and why? What can you do to further that relationship and grow it to the next stage?

14

THE IDOL OF IMAGE

"Your beauty should not come from outward adornment, such as elaborate hairstyles and the wearing of gold jewelry or fine clothes. Rather, it should be that of your inner self, the unfading beauty of a gentle and quiet spirit, which is of great worth in God's sight."

—1 Peter 3:3-4 (NIV)

The music industry is insanely image-based. People inside the industry don't want to admit this, but a simple look around will confirm the obvious. Just how many obese vocalists do you see fronting a popular band? Larger bands—whether male or female dominated—are fashionable and put together. I've never been that guy, however, and it's eaten me up. At five- nine and 159 pounds, I'm average at best. I don't even follow rock or metal trends, because I don't have a single piercing or tattoo. So when our band struggles with sales or shows, I blame myself for not being good-looking, taller, or well-dressed. This mindset has led to a lot of confidence and identity issues, especially within the last year.

I know what to do to change my appearance. I could go to the gym three or four times a week to gain muscle and look better, but I also recognize that exercise won't make me taller, my forehead smaller, or my beard fuller. Such mindsets of acceptance based on appearance are toxic and affected my day-to-day. I wouldn't go to certain events because I felt down about my appearance. It affected my friendships and my ability to do the things normal people do. Couple this insecurity with social anxiety, and you have a devastating combo.

Though this may sound odd, my insecurity affected my faith. Deep within my subconscious, I believe I harbored resentment against God for my physical appearance. I found it hard to love myself, because I don't look the way I want. This obsession with my appearance impeded something bigger, though. We all have things in our life we can't control, and that's not God's fault. We are products of free will. I can't force anyone to love me. Instead, that has to be their decision. As much as I want people to like me or my music, that's ultimately their choice, and I can't control the outcome. There are, however, things I can control. Mainly, how I deal with the cards life has given me. As you can see, I've played a poor hand of cards, believing appearance determines worth. Ninety percent of us will never be fully content with our looks, but we can control how we respond to the cards we've been dealt.

In this passage of Scripture, we're told true beauty is not external, but internal. A "gentle and quiet spirit" is worth more than being known just because you're super hot. Had I spent my time focusing on being gentle, humble, and caring for others, as opposed to feeling sorry for myself, I wouldn't just be impacting others for good, but I also would feel better about myself. God would use me to spread his love—which is true beauty—instead of caring about my hair or what other people think of my clothes.

There's something about people who are kind and gentle in a world full of outrage and anger. We notice it more than someone's appearance, because those traits are so rare. While it's hard to admit my obsession with my looks (as I've never spoke about this till now), I want to be the type of man known for these traits and to find my worth in God's eyes, rather than worrying about my appearance and living in anxiety and fear.

What will it take for us to recognize God's beauty in a quiet spirit over what the world tells us? What's better? Vanity? Or gentleness? I know what I'd choose.

DAY 14 REFLECTION

1. Have you ever wanted to change your appearance or something physical on your body? If so, why? Did you wish God had made you look different? Have you been able to reconcile that?
2. Have you ever known someone who's beautiful because of their gentleness and humility? What about them stood out? How did they emulate God's love?

15

OF JUDGMENT, SLANDER, AND GRACE

"Brothers and sisters, do not slander one another. Anyone who speaks against a brother or sister or judges them speaks against the law and judges it. When you judge the law, you are not keeping it, but sitting in judgment on it. There is only one Lawgiver and Judge, the one who is able to save and destroy. But you—who are you to judge your neighbor?"
—James 4:11-12 (NIV)

Love. This one word conjures up emotions for everyone, from the most devout Christian to the secular humanist. Love is preached consistently throughout the Bible and reflected in the words and actions of Jesus; yet love seems to be the one thing Christians—including myself—have a tough time grasping. Instead, we're quite good at judging others.

Throughout most of my life, whether face-to-face or behind closed doors, I judged people for their actions. I was quick to call out when a person was committing sin. After all, that's what God wanted, right? For me to hold other people accountable to his standards? But how often has shame, judgement, and condemnation led to someone changing? How often do they experience love through those actions?

In this passage of Scripture, it's easy to see how judging people speaks evil of them, whereas it's God's role to hold them accountable for their actions. Instead, verses like Ephesians 4:32 (ESV) remind us we are to "Be kind to one another, tenderhearted, forgiving one another, as God in Christ forgave you." No one ever feels good when they're condemned for their actions, no matter how wrong they are.

Sometimes times we get judged by Christians because their faith has become a bludgeoning weapon. I know this from personal experience; one church protested us during a tour with Born of Osiris.

A lot of these attitudes stem from our competitive nature or wanting to one-up each other. While we may have graduated high school and that system of drama, we still like to show off our life accomplishments to signal we're better than others. As I mentioned in a prior day's devotion, my competitive nature caused me to want to one-up other people. What better way was there to do that than using the Bible as a tool to judge someone? I was quick to pass judgement, convinced by other Christians that this was our role—to point out the glaring inconsistencies in the lives of those who are falling short (see James 7:24).

Don't get me wrong: Christians *are* called to give "righteous judgement." But was that what I was practicing?

Verse after verse, from Galatians 5 to Ephesians 4, remind us to do so in love and gentleness, hoping that conviction, *not* condemnation, occurs. Instead, I would turn up my nose at those sleeping with their girlfriends, all while I had sin patterns of my own.

So what is righteous judgement, and how can we break the cycle of trying to play God by judging others? The best example I can give you is that of Christ on the cross. While we were still enemies, he laid down his life so we might find ours. God righteously judged Christ, and Christ loved us enough not inflict the penalty we were due for our sins.

Are we judging others with that same love? A love that would have us die if it meant our enemies would transform their hearts?

We need to ensure when we "judge" others that it comes from no other place than love. To do anything besides that is just slandering a brother or sister.

DAY 15 REFLECTION

1. Have you ever found yourself thinking you're better than someone else who made a mistake or whose actions you disagree with? How can you instead see them through Christ's eyes and love them to the point they would experience conviction?

2. Think about the last time you messed up. How would you have wanted people to treat you? With mercy? Or judgment? What are some techniques you can use to see people as being in the same fallen state as you, so that you can offer grace when they stumble? Write down a few ideas, then act on them.

16

ITCHING EARS AND SECONDARY PASSIONS

"For the time is coming when people will not endure sound teaching, but having itching ears they will accumulate for themselves teachers to suit their own passions."

—2 Timothy 4:3 (ESV)

We tend to think Christian morals are going straight down the drain in our modern era. We point to false teachers and people being led astray by every new wind of doctrine. Yet, history tells a different story.

Right after Jesus was resurrected, the Apostle Paul had to call out the Judaizers who taught that someone could only become a Christian if they were circumcised (see Galatians 1:6-2:21 and Acts 15). Later, Gnostic Christians engaged in orgies and sex rituals. Prior to the Reformation, the Roman Catholic church sold indulgences so people could pay for their deceased family members to get out of hell. From there, churches divided over baptism, predestination, and church membership. We like to pretend that only *now* we've gone off the rails, but that's hardly the case.

While playing a music festival in Midland, Texas, called "Rock The Desert," I began a conversation about this topic with another musician. Rock The Desert is a Christian event, and I've always felt out of place at festivals like that. We're usually one of the few metal bands, while everyone else are worship artists. The crowd is also eclectic; some even subscribe to the idea that "Monster energy drinks are part of Satan's plan to corrupt our households." (Watch the YouTube video on this. It's awesome in all the wrong ways.) Throughout the crowd—and even among the musicians playing—there are a lot of differing beliefs.

As the other musician and I talked, examples of those odd differences popped up, like those who believe dancing is forbidden (despite David dancing before the Lord), that women can only wear long dresses, or that holding snakes is a way to show your trust in God.

It's odd that we abandon the gospel and divide over such secondary issues. One church may forbid dancing but condemn "God loving everyone" as heretical because of others' sins.

Instead of sound doctrine—that Christ died, resurrected, and is coming again—we find teachers to suit our passions and harp on them in the name of morality or politics. This is far too easy to spot. Instead of preaching the gospel and God's great love for humanity, a pastor will spend an entire sermon on the sinfulness of premarital sex, yet himself be overweight in the pulpit. He may even go to lunch after the sermon and gorge himself at the Golden Corral, thinking nothing of it, yet believing his doctrine is sound. People who align with him and his bias may flock to his church because they can point their fingers at others instead of recognizing where they're falling short. Their itching ears tickled, they never have to deal with their own brokenness.

The hard part, however, is that we all have biases and itching ears. If we don't cling fast to the words and teachings of Jesus, we might judge and condemn others and divide over silly issues while never examining ourselves. Each day we must remind ourselves of what matters most. As the Apostle Paul states in 1 Corinthians 15, the Gospel is of first importance. Cling to it. Don't be led astray by itching ears and your passions.

DAY 16 REFLECTION

1. Write a list of beliefs you have about life or even biblical doctrine. Examples can include: Jesus was God. The earth was created in eight days (or eight billion years). Or even your views on premarital sex, politics, or predestination. Cover a lot of ground, and make a list with at least fifteen items on it.

2. Now review your list and pick which issues are secondary, that Christians divide over. Pick the ones we're unified on. If you feel uncertain, review 1 Corinthians 15:1-11, where Paul states what is of utmost importance in our doctrine. How many of your beliefs were secondary? How can you focus on the gospel instead?

17

FOOLISH DOGMA

"Come, let us sing for joy to the Lord; let us shout aloud to the Rock of our salvation."
—Psalm 95:1 (NIV)

"My parents won't support me because they said metal is devil music."

I've heard this statement uttered by fans more times than I care to count. Oddly, it outnumbers by a good margin the stories fans tell me of tragedy or mental illness. This alone has been difficult to comprehend. Why are hordes of young adults crushed by their parents' views on a style of music they want to pursue? I believe there's something important parents forget, especially in how their children's view of faith is often shaped by their influence. If you'll remember from earlier devotions, our view of God and personal biases can affect our interpretation of Scripture and land us in the realm of foolish dogma, as opposed to biblical truth.

Many fans I meet are hungry to play metal music, but their Christian parents remain unsupportive. While their kids see it as an outlet to praise God through their passion, the parents can only hear the screaming or associate the style with the "demonic." Because their parents remained unmoved, the issues it causes their children can last a lifetime. I've seen a lot of depression and mental health problems in fans ranging from teens to older adults because their parents struck down their God-given passions.

On one hand, it's easy to understand a parent not wanting their fifteen-year-old son to write lyrics with curse words in the middle of a heavy breakdown. But on the other, if they want to write music in a certain style, why would we assume one style is more pleasing to God than another? Isn't God the author of music *and* creativity?

Even the organization I'm writing this devotional for—HeartSupport—has caught flack for being Christians and supporting metal music. What they remind people of is that there's no difference between the sacred and secular. Because God created all things, music—by its very nature—is holy. So if God created the universe, then he would have had to create music, right? Thus, what people do with music is up to them. What people do with food is also their decision. They can use it for good, or it can be detrimental. People can use a style of music to build people up, or to tear them down. So when parents believe their children can't make a joyful noise and shout to God like the Psalmist proclaims, using metal music, they've wandered into myth.

Besides, there's no such thing as "Christian" music, anyway. Music doesn't have a soul, so it cannot be saved. *Only people can.* "Christian" is just a label, the same way "metal" is.

We must also remember God puts desires, gifts, and talents in our hearts. When I was a teenager, I wrote songs I didn't want to write because I thought the songs I *wanted* to write would anger my parents. So who was I actually trying to please? God? Or my parents? When the Psalmist says to shout before the Lord and sing, he doesn't say, "But you can only sing hymns." Nor does he say only rap, pop, or jazz is allowed. He just says to sing and make it joyful before the Lord.

So the next time you hear someone using Jesus as a means to label his creation evil, remind them he created the entire Earth *and* music. And just maybe he's using his creation to save people in the metal scene.

DAY 17 REFLECTION

1. Has anyone ever told you something that God would say is good, is actually bad? Examples include sex, food, music, etc. How would God view his creation, and how should you—in turn—think about his creation and use it to glorify him?
2. What passions has God laid in your heart? Have you been discouraged against following them? If so, why and how can you correct that?

18

REFLECTIONS ON "UNWHOLESOME TALK"

"Do not let any unwholesome talk come out of your mouths, but only what is helpful for building others up according to their needs, that it may benefit those who listen."
—Ephesians 4:29 (NIV)

If you'll remember back to my time at the music festival in Midland, Texas, one conversation I had was about "cursing being forbidden in the Bible." If you've read Jake Luhrs' devotional, *Mountains*, you probably remember how he came hot out of the gate with curse words in a devotional. There weren't many, and he didn't do it to be cool or edgy, but to tell stories as they happened. I agreed with Jake and the biblical interpretations he introduced in the preface as a forewarning, but I feel I should expand more on the topic in this devotional.

During my conversation at the festival, we debated whether we would allow our children to watch R-rated movies. My opinion was that as long as curse words were the worst thing happening on screen, I wouldn't care all that much, because cursing isn't a sin—depending on the context, of course. The other individual didn't agree and immediately used the Scripture we're reviewing today as the ammunition for his argument. I expected that to be the case, as Christians often use this verse as the trump card on the issue.

"Unwholesome", however, is subjective. What may be unwholesome to someone in the Deep South may be very different to someone from Philadelphia. In some parts of the Middle East, they consider the thumbs-up symbol to be equivalent to holding up the middle finger. We can talk about hell in church, but when someone says, "What the hell," some find that offensive.

What the Bible is clear about, however, is that we must not tear others down with our words or slander them. Jesus talks about it (Matthew 5:22), as does his half-brother James (James 3:9-10). The Proverbs also point out that those who slander are fools (10:18).

I'd wager most of us are guilty of tearing others down with our words. I know I certainly am.

It makes one wonder: Is it worse to stub your toe and exclaim, "Shit!" in pain? Or to gossip and tear down someone else made in the image of God? Before I began to know God's heart and his love for people, I would have said curse words were worse. That's what a religious heart will do to you.

So what on Earth does this verse mean? Taking context into the situation, the Apostle Paul reminds us that our talk needs to benefit others by building up and not tearing down. Sometimes a coarse word may cause uncontrollable laughter for a friend who is grieving. Other times it may be wholly inappropriate for a grieving friend. The point, though, is that we must take into consideration how we build people up with our words, as opposed to getting hung up on a word while we slander and judge others because of their language.

Remember that Jesus sat and ate with the very people whose language probably rivaled sailors (his disciples were fishermen, after all). Never once do we hear him condemn them, but instead he engages their hearts. We must do the same.

DAY 18 REFLECTION

1. If you've found yourself using coarse language, ask yourself why you do it. Does it build someone up? Or would it offend them? How can you seek the Lord's heart in using wisdom regarding the issue?
2. Think of a time when someone called you a name. How did you feel? Did they use expletives with it? Review the times you've heard coarse joking or unwholesome talk and when it's offended you. Were you offended by the language, or because it was hurtful? If you recognize it's because it hurt you, how can you instead offer compassion with kind words when you're angry?

19

LIKE-MINDED

"Finally, all of you, be like-minded, be sympathetic, love one another, be compassionate and humble."
—1 Peter 3:8 (NIV)

The other month, a friend of mine told me about his new church and how kind everyone there was. We like to tease, but I made a jab at him to challenge the notion of what acceptance looks like inside a church.

"Oh, yeah?" I said. "Have you told them you're gay yet?"

This wasn't by any means a shot at his sexuality, but rather to see how vulnerable he'd been with them.

I don't bring up this incident to incite arguments about homosexuality and sin. I could have said, "Did you tell them you're divorced or drink alcohol?" and there would be a Christian somewhere who would want to judge that person. Most people inside the church look pretty and play a role instead of being known for sympathy and compassion toward hurting men and women.

For some, the trouble point in this verse is the word "like-minded," which they assume means that we all must agree on the same secondary doctrine or which translation of the Bible to use, or that we must have the same political leanings.

Instead, we are to be like-minded in the way we love people: compassionate and humble in our interactions. Our goal as Christians—above all else—should be to show the love of God to others in the personhood of Jesus. Everyone likes Jesus, but no one seems to like many of his followers. This is mainly because we force Scripture down people's throats or snidely debate atheists on the internet. If we were of a like mind, we would be sympathetic, loving those inside the church and outside it. Grace changes people, *not* shame or an agenda.

Speaking of an agenda, a few months ago someone messaged me on Facebook. They wanted their agenda forced onto non-believers through my influence. In the message, they requested I find a band we were playing a festival with and ensure they "came to Christ."

When I say "requested," that's putting it mildly. Instead, it was more militant and along the lines of, "This is your duty."

I'm a firm believer that we don't bring anyone to Christ, but that Christ himself woos us. If we had the power to save someone, then we would be God, right? Instead, we show and carry the message, and God himself brings them into his kingdom. Second, I sincerely doubt that if my first and only interaction with an individual was, "Please accept Christ into your heart," then that conversation would push them further away. If following Jesus means you pester and annoy strangers, then I doubt anyone wants to be part of the club.

From what I've experienced, the most effective way to introduce people to Christ is to love them relentlessly. When you love, and love, and keep loving them, despite their failures, shortcomings, and missteps, people will wonder why you do that. They may sit back and think, "Why is he so kind in a world that's so dark? I want whatever he has." The steps are slow and deliberate and must happen on their time.

We don't need more cultural converts who pray a prayer and never live "like-minded" or like Jesus. If we force conversion, we'll create fakes or turn men and women away. We need humble, compassionate followers of the risen Messiah. If we are like-minded in that manner, we can watch the world change.

DAY 19 REFLECTION

1. Have you ever forced someone to do something? How did it turn out? Good or bad?
2. How do you reach people with your faith? Are you "like-minded" and walking in humility and compassion? Would they be receptive to you? If not, why?

20

BLIND GUIDES

"Leave them; they are blind guides. If the blind lead the blind, both will fall into a pit."

—Matthew 15:14 (NIV)

If you're wondering how we've made it through this devotional without bringing up politics, you're about to be sorely disappointed. It's not a shock that the West is becoming less religious, along with a rapid decline in church attendance. Our modern mantra is even, "You do you." Some believe this is the source of the problems we're experiencing, as hate and vitriol saturate our news.

However, I believe the problem stems from us following blind guides. Look around. How many people are obsessed with politics and political solutions to fix our problems? We've elevated politicians to a God-like level, expecting them to save us, and continue to shove them into the gaping hole reserved for God. People can't even see their own blindness and idolatry, and it's insane. Republicans support President Trump for doing things they ripped President Obama for.

Democrats have destroyed President Trump for something they praised President Clinton for. We take flawed, and often less than reputable men and women, and give them our undying loyalty. *It's wicked.*

Don't think I'm saying we need a theocracy, where the answer is for a religion to run the government. History will confirm that's a terrible idea. Separation of church and state is important, especially since Jesus's kingdom will never look like a man-made government. And government should honor our freedom to choose faith freely.

But the way in which we've elevated our political leaders to messiahs is leading many away from *true* faith. Their faith is now in politics, and it's the blind leading the blind, as Jesus says. What's interesting in this passage is that Jesus was referring to a religious and political ruling class known as the Pharisees. They mixed their faith with politics, and Jesus over and over refers to them as blind guides, dead men's bones, vipers, whitewashed tombs, and children of hell (Matthew 23). When we follow leaders like these, it will lead to nothing but destruction.

We should reevaluate who's truly leading our lives and who we worship. Many men and women have cried over a politician losing or become depressed over legislation. They've become fearful and anxious about the future, and yet the real Messiah says he gives his followers peace and joy. So who are they *really* worshipping?

We must look to God instead of worshipping those in power. Remember that politicians are imperfect, whereas Jesus is perfect. Don't fall into the pit. Open your eyes and follow the one who will lead you to truth, joy, and peace.

DAY 20 REFLECTION

1. Have you recently found yourself outraged over politics or political news? Do you struggle to find peace and joy? If so, why?
2. Remember that Jesus tells his followers that in this world they'll have trouble, but that he's overcome the world and will bring peace into their lives (John 16:33). How can you learn to trust God and find peace, even when the world around us seems to burn?

21

WILLFUL PRAYER

"This is the confidence we have in approaching God: that if we ask anything according to his will, he hears us."
   —1 John 5:14 (NIV)

Today we reach the final day of our three-week journey together. I've done my best to provide you with clarity and knowledge. In studying for this book, I've learned a lot through self-reflection and even sitting in contemplation over key verses.

This last verse I specifically saved for today, as I believe its subject is essential for following Jesus: *prayer.* Prayer isn't something I'm very good at, and I think it's because it's something most of us misunderstand.

Ten years ago, doctors diagnosed my dad with esophageal cancer. As his son, the news devastated me. I was at that awkward stage in life, being on the cusp of adulthood, where I understood what was happening, but my brain kept me in denial and playing out "what-ifs."

As a kid raised in church, I did the only thing I knew to—

I prayed. I prayed *a lot*. But I felt guilty praying, because I rarely ever made it a practice. Instead, when I *did* pray, it was to ask God for a favor, kind of like that random family member who pops over only when they need money.

When I went to see my dad before his surgery to remove the cancer, he said something that has always stuck with me. He said, "Don't pray for healing. Just pray that whatever happens, God uses it for his purpose."

There was nothing but complete peace in his eyes, and no matter how the operation turned out, my dad had accepted his fate. Fortunately, doctors were able to remove the cancer, and it's never returned.

Dwelling on this moment in my life, I wanted to dig deeper to understand what my dad meant when he uttered those words. In 1 John 5:14, the portion of the verse that stood out to me is, "if we ask anything according to his will."

We always pray for something—to get that new job, to meet our soulmate, to get out of a financial bind, or for an illness to go away. But what if the way we pray is actually selfish? What if none of what we're praying for is part of God's plan? This can be a frustrating question for Christians and non-believers alike. We don't feel like God is hearing us or honoring our prayers. We believe we know best, but perhaps God is telling us, "Be patient. Trust me. This will all work out in the end."

You may think, "That's easy for you to say! But what if your dad died? How would have *that* worked out in the end?" Honestly, the more I reflect on the question, the reply I've come up with is this: *What if the way he handled his death— with his faith never wavering—brought one person to Christ at that hospital?* That would be one more person in eternity, and my dad would already be there.

We'll never understand God's ultimate plan, but we know he's good and trustworthy.

Prayer changes things, but even the best things we pray for might not be best for everyone. Instead, perhaps the greatest question God asks us repeatedly throughout Scripture, prayer, and our lives is simple: *Do you trust me?*

DAY 21 REFLECTION

1. Do you pray? If so, how much, and in what ways do you pray? If you struggle to pray, consider going line by line through the Lord's Prayer (Matthew 6:9-11) to format your needs, praise him, and ask for forgiveness.

2. What is the hardest area of your life in which you find yourself unwilling to trust God? How can you turn your will and way over into his care?

ABOUT THE AUTHOR

Ryan Kirby is the lead singer of the American metalcore band, Fit For A King. To date the band has toured over 20 countries and sold over 100,000 albums in the United States and abroad. When not on tour, Ryan spends his time as a sports enthusiast, passionately watching the Dallas Cowboys, Mavericks, and Texas Rangers. He (obviously) lives in Texas with his wife, Crystal, and two fur babies.

 twitter.com/ryankirbz

 instagram.com/ryankirbz

ABOUT HEARTSUPPORT

HeartSupport was created by Grammy-nominated musician Jake Luhrs of metal band August Burns Red. After seeing his fans struggling through the same issues and addictions he went through growing up, he wanted to use his platform to impact a generation. In 2016, the organization won a Philanthropy Award in recognition of their work at the Alternative Press Music Awards. In 2017, the organization was recognized as one of the top 100 nonprofits in the world for social innovation. The team at HeartSupport often travels around the United States educating churches, nonprofits, and other organizations, while weaving engaging content along with statistics to inform and train their audiences regarding issues facing today's generation.

facebook.com/hearsupport

twitter.com/heartsupport

instagram.com/heartsupport

Also By HeartSupport

MOUNTAINS

25 DEVOTIONALS WITH JAKE LUHRS

Christian books often avoid talking about real struggles. It's time to change that.

Mountains is a devotional for men and women who want to hear real stories of faith, struggle, defeat, and wins but are tired of Christian cliches and platitudes. Follow Grammy-nominated musician, Jake Luhrs of August Burns Red, as he guides you through the mountains he's faced in life, and how he came out stronger in his relationship with God.

Along the way, he'll encourage you to face your demons, keep the faith, grow in love, and fight to reach the top with twenty-five handpicked Scriptures which encouraged him through his darkest valleys.

Gear up. **It's time to face your mountains.**

D W A R F P L A N E T

A PRACTICAL GUIDE THROUGH DEPRESSION

Depression feels like living on a distant dwarf planet. This book is your way out.

You know the feeling. You're in a cold, lifeless place, and all alone on the fringes of the solar system. Sure, you can see the sun from afar and know other people are having the time of their life, but you're stuck on this dwarf planet of an illness no one cares about.

That ends now. This book is the result of years of coaching, studying, winning, failing, and talking to hundreds of people. Coming from an organization that's been named one of the top 100 non-profits in the realm of mental health, we'll help you discover a hopeful future. Inside these pages, you'll explore new facts about your depression and navigate obstacles that stand in the way.

If you're tired of trite books that read like medical dictionaries and want authentic and vulnerable storytelling, *Dwarf Planet* is the escape pod you've been looking for. You'll complete exercises that challenge you, read stories that inspire you, and finally feel like someone understands your struggle.

Climb in. **We're going to get you off this rock.**

Also By HeartSupport

THE JOURNEY FROM SELF-HARM
TO HEALING

Most self-harm books are filled with medical terminology that reads like a dictionary, leaving those who suffer all the more confused. They're uncertain how to ask for support or talk about the shame they feel. Many are uncertain even why they do it. All they know is it helps.

ReWrite is a book that cuts through the clutter and platitudes to help those who cut and their friends and family understand:

- The stigmas and the truth behind self-harm
- Reasons you began self-injury even when you're unsure
- How to cope with the guilt and shame
- Tried-and-true recovery techniques and exercises
- How a person's faith can help
- Information and excursuses for friends and family who want to support their loved one

Don't waste another day stuck in the clutches of self-harm. Join others who have successfully turned their lives around with information provided here.

Step into the journey. ReWrite your story.